Pebble® Plus
Bilingüe/ Bilingual

RAMAS MILITARES/MILITARY BRANCHES

LA ARMADA DE EE.UU. /
THE U.S. NAVY

por/by Jennifer Reed

Editor Consultor/Consulting Editor: Dra. Gail Saunders-Smith

CAPSTONE PRESS
a capstone imprint

Pebble Plus is published by Capstone Press,
151 Good Counsel Drive, P.O. Box 669, Mankato, Minnesota 56002.
www.capstonepress.com

092009
005618CGS10

 Books published by Capstone Press are manufactured with paper
containing at least 10 percent post-consumer waste.

Library of Congress Cataloging-in-Publication Data
Reed, Jennifer, 1967–
   [U.S. Navy. Spanish & English]
   La Armada de EE.UU. / por Jennifer Reed = The U.S. Navy / by Jennifer Reed.
   p. cm. — (Pebble Plus bilingüe/bilingual. Ramas militares = Military branches)
   Includes index.
   Summary: "Simple text and photographs describe the U.S. Navy's purpose, jobs, and ships — in both
English and Spanish" — Provided by publisher.
   ISBN 978-1-4296-4604-8 (library binding)
   1. United States. Navy — Juvenile literature. I. Title. II. Title: U.S. Navy.
VA58.4.R4418 2010
359.00973 — dc22   2009030381

Editorial Credits
Gillia Olson, editor; Strictly Spanish, translation services; Katy Kudela, bilingual editor; Renée T. Doyle,
   designer; Jo Miller, photo researcher; Eric Manske, production specialist

Photo Credits
Capstone Press/Karon Dubke, 3
DVIC/General Dynamics Electric Boat, 19
Photo courtesy of Northrop Grumman Ship Systems, 1
Shutterstock/Derek Gordon, 11
U.S. Navy Photo by MC1 James E. Foehl, back cover, 22; by MC1 William R. Goodwin, 21; by MC2 Lolita Lewis,
   front cover; by MC2 Ron Reeves, 15; by MC3 Jason A. Johnston, 9; by MCSN Aaron Holt, 7; by PH2 Eric S.
   Logsdon, 13; by PH3 Douglas G. Morrison, 17; by PHAN Eben Boothby, 5

Artistic Effects
iStockphoto/Piotr Przeszlo, metal treatment, cover, 1
iStockphoto/walrusmail, rivets on metal, front and back cover, 1, 24

Capstone Press thanks Dr. Sarandis Papadopoulos, Naval Historian, for his assistance with this book.

Note to Parents and Teachers

The Ramas militares/Military Branches set supports national science standards related
to science, technology, and society. This book describes and illustrates the U.S. Navy in
both English and Spanish. The images support early readers in understanding the text.
The repetition of words and phrases helps early readers learn new words. This book also
introduces early readers to subject-specific vocabulary words, which are defined in the
Glossary section. Early readers may need assistance to read some words and to use the
Table of Contents, Glossary, Internet Sites, and Index sections of the book.

Table of Contents

Tabla de contenidos

What Is the Navy?

The Navy is a branch of the United States Armed Forces. The Navy guards the sea to keep the country safe.

¿Qué es la Armada?

La Armada es una rama de las Fuerzas Armadas de Estados Unidos. La Armada custodia los mares para mantener la seguridad del país.

4

Navy Jobs

All people in the Navy are called sailors. Some sailors are navigators. They plan which way Navy ships will travel.

Trabajos en la Armada

Todas las personas de la Armada son llamadas marineros. Algunos marineros son navegantes. Ellos planifican hacia dónde navegarán los buques de la Armada.

Some sailors are mechanics.

They fix machines.

Algunos marineros son mecánicos.

Ellos reparan máquinas.

Navy pilots fly airplanes.
Air controllers tell pilots
when to take off and land.

Los pilotos de la Armada vuelan
aviones. Los controladores aéreos
les dicen a los pilotos cuándo
despegar y aterrizar.

The Navy has special forces. Navy SEALs are trained to fight on land and sea. Underwater, Navy divers fix ships and search the ocean.

La Armada tiene fuerzas especiales. Los Navy SEALs están entrenados para combatir en tierra y mar. Bajo agua, los buzos de la Armada reparan buques y hacen búsquedas por el océano.

Navy SEALs

Navy Ships

Aircraft carriers are

the largest Navy ships.

They are floating airports.

Buques de la Armada

Los portaaviones son los buques

más grandes de la Armada.

Son aeropuertos flotantes.

Destroyers and cruisers are
warships. They shoot large
guns and missiles.

Los destructores y cruceros son
buques de guerra. Ellos disparan
grandes cañones y misiles.

Submarines travel underwater.
They fire underwater missiles
called torpedoes.

Los submarinos viajan bajo
el agua. Ellos disparan misiles
subacuáticos llamados torpedos.

Keeping Us Safe

The brave sailors of the

Navy protect our country.

Their teamwork keeps us safe.

Mantener nuestra seguridad

Los valientes marineros de

la Armada protegen a nuestro

país. Su trabajo en equipo

nos mantiene seguros.

Glossary

Armed Forces — the whole military; the U.S. Armed Forces include the Army, Navy, Air Force, Marine Corps, and Coast Guard.

branch — a part of a larger group

guard — to watch over

missile — a weapon that is fired at a target to blow it up

SEALs — a special forces group in the Navy; SEALs stands for SEa, Air, and Land.

special forces — groups trained for very difficult and dangerous jobs in the Navy

torpedo — an underwater missile used to blow up a target

warship — a Navy ship used mainly to fight enemies

Internet Sites

FactHound offers a safe, fun way to find Internet sites related to this book. All of the sites on FactHound have been researched by our staff.

Here's all you do:

Visit *www.facthound.com*

FactHound will fetch the best sites for you!

Glosario

el buque de guerra — un barco de la Armada que se usa para batallar contra los enemigos

las Fuerzas Armadas — todas las ramas militares; las Fuerzas Armadas de EE.UU. incluyen el Ejército, la Armada, la Fuerza Aérea, la Infantería de Marina y la Guardia Costera.

las fuerzas especiales — grupos entrenados para trabajos muy difíciles y peligrosos en la Armada

guardar — cuidar de algo/alguien

el misil — un arma grande que se lanza para hacer explotar un objetivo

la rama — una parte de un grupo más grande

los SEALs — un grupo de fuerzas especiales de la Armada, SEALs significa en inglés Sea (mar), Air (aire) y Land (tierra).

el torpedo — un misil subacuático que se usa para hacer explotar un objetivo

Sitios de Internet

FactHound brinda una forma segura y divertida de encontrar sitios de Internet relacionados con este libro. Todos los sitios en FactHound han sido investigados por nuestro personal.

Esto es todo lo que tú necesitas hacer:

Visita *www.facthound.com*

¡FactHound buscará los mejores sitios para ti!

Index

Índice